Scholastic Canada Bi...

CANADIAN PIONEERS

Maxine Trottier

illustrated by

Alan & Lea Daniel

	DATE DUE		

Scholastic Canada Ltd.
Toronto New York London Auckland Sydney
Mexico City New Delhi Hong Kong Buenos Aires

For those who came before us . . .
Pour ceux et celles qui nous ont précédés

– M.T.

Photo Credits

Page 6: Samuel de Champlain, *Habitation de Québec*, National Archives of Canada C-009711
Page 23: J.E. Laughlin, *Crossing the Stream, Ontario – Loyalist Pioneers*, National Archives of Canada C-013992
Page 34: unknown artist, *Canadian Log-House*, National Archives of Canada C-006753
Page 36: *Belleville, looking east, 1830*, Archives of Ontario, Thomas Burrowes fonds C 1-0-0-0-110. I0002229
Page 37: Susanna Moodie, *Goldfinch and Thistle*, National Library of Canada NL-15558
Page 38: unknown artist, *Free Farms for the Million*, ca. 1890, National Archives of Canada C-063482 (text at base superimposed from C-063478)
Page 46: Yousef Karsh, *Wasyl Eleniak*, 4 Jan, 1947, National Archives of Canada PA-211301

Map by Paul Dotey

The author would like to thank Peter Cazaly and Larry Lozon for their help with things British and military.

National Library of Canada Cataloguing in Publication

Trottier, Maxine
Canadian pioneers / Maxine Trottier ; illustrations by Alan and Lea Daniel.

(Scholastic Canada biographies)
For children aged 6-9.
ISBN 0-7791-1405-1

1. Pioneers--Canada--Biography--Juvenile literature. 2. Frontier and pioneer life--Canada--Juvenile literature. I. Daniel, Alan, 1939- II. Title. III. Series.

FC25.T77 2003   j971'.009'9   C2003-901008-2

6 5 4 3   Printed in Canada   04 05 06 07

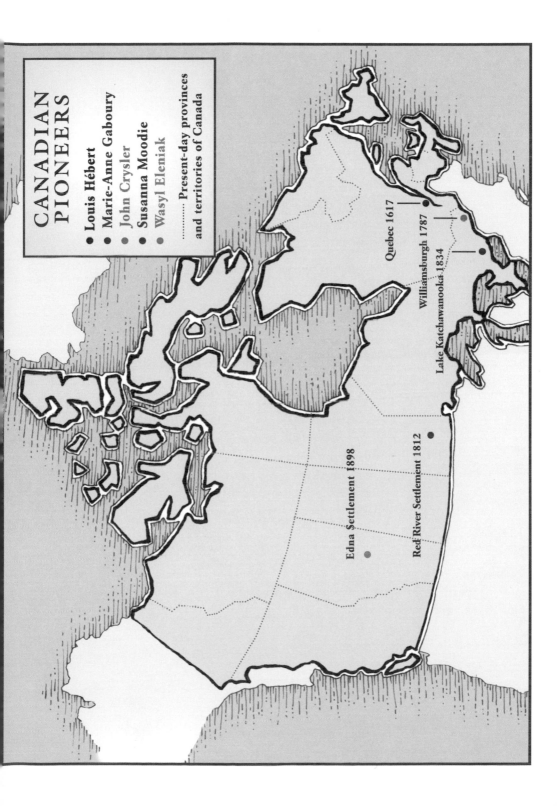

CANADIAN PIONEERS

- Louis Hébert
- Marie-Anne Gaboury
- John Crysler
- Susanna Moodie
- Wasyl Eleniak
...... Present-day provinces and territories of Canada

Quebec 1617

Williamsburgh 1787

Lake Katchawanooka 1834

Edna Settlement 1898

Red River Settlement 1812

Louis Hébert
The First *Habitant*

Long ago in faraway France, a man named Louis had a garden near the Seine River. There were many other gardens coming to life that spring of 1617, but Louis Hébert's was special. Like his father before him, Louis was an apothecary — a man who made medicines. His Paris garden was filled with pennyroyal and lavender, chamomile and thyme, and many other herbs and plants that he used to create his medicines.

Louis had always been interested in growing things. Little did he know that one day his interest would take him on a grand adventure to New France.

Louis Hébert had gone to New France twice before, once with his wife, Marie. He had worked as an apothecary at the French settlement of Port-Royal, where he met the explorer Samuel de Champlain. But the Héberts had returned to France, and Champlain had moved on to start a new settlement at Quebec on the St. Lawrence River.

Now Champlain was back in Paris. With the Hurons bringing their furs to trade, his Quebec colony was doing well enough. But Champlain, working with a company of fur-trading merchants in France, believed the settlement needed to be more than just a trading post. He was in Paris to recruit people for his colony in New France.

In Paris, Champlain made Louis Hébert a wonderful offer. Quebec needed someone who could look after the health of the soldiers, traders and priests who were working there. He promised that Louis would receive 200 *livres* a year as his salary. The company of French merchants would provide Louis and his family with supplies, food and shelter.

Louis Hébert had been born in Paris. It was his

home and the home of his family. But here was a chance to own his own land and to be independent. He signed the contract that Champlain offered. The Héberts would be the first family to arrive in New France.

Louis Hébert sold his house and shop. Then he, his wife and their three children, Guillaume, Anne and Guillemette, set out for the port of Honfleur.

But when they arrived at their ship, the *Sainte-Étienne,* Louis received terrible news. They would not be allowed to board unless he signed a different contract. He was told that Champlain did not have the power to make his offer. Louis Hébert's wages would be cut to 100 *livres* a year for three years. After that, he could work only for the company, and for no wages at all. He would not be allowed to trade furs, and whatever crops he grew must be sold to the company at the price they decided.

Louis Hébert felt he had no choice. He signed the unfair contract and set sail with his family for New France.

The voyage across the Atlantic took three months. When the Héberts finally arrived at Quebec on July 15, they saw a world that was very different from what they had known in Paris. The settlement that Champlain called the Habitation was at the bottom of a steep hill. The buildings were surrounded by a palisade, and beyond that lay a wilderness of thick forests.

But where trees grew, so could crops. Louis Hébert claimed a piece of land on the hill above the Habitation. The work of clearing the land was a long, difficult task, and Hébert had only his family to help him. Since there was no

Samuel de Champlain's engraving of the Habitation (1608)

school at Quebec, the children could work with their parents. One by one the trees were chopped down and cut up. Then the stumps were slowly burned and pulled out of the soil. Any stones had to be removed and set aside in piles. With the stones Louis Hébert would later build a house, the first one to stand on the hill overlooking Quebec.

There were no plows in New France, since there were no horses to pull them, so Hébert dug his land with a spade. The work went very slowly, but when Champlain came back to New France in 1618 he saw that Hébert had made great progress. The soil was good here, and he again had a garden. His work as an apothecary kept Hébert very busy, but still he managed to grow cabbage, turnips, lettuce and parsley. He also planted wheat and corn. Besides the herbs he had used in France, Hébert probably grew healing plants shown to him by the Micmac at Port-Royal — boneset for fevers, Jack-in-the-pulpit for stomach aches, and golden seal for bleeding and skin sores.

Over the years Louis Hébert planted an apple orchard and grew Normandy apples. He tended grapes in a vineyard. He raised cows and pigs to

provide the family with milk and meat. No one else was doing such things. The people at Quebec continued to depend mostly upon the group of merchants in France for supplies.

It took a long time for the company to realize the good work that Louis Hébert was doing. All they were interested in was the fur trade. In time, though, their opinion changed. In 1621 Hébert was made a court official for the king, and in 1623 the land he had been farming was put into his name. Three years later Louis Hébert was given another piece of land, on the St. Charles River near Quebec, and the title of Sieur de l'Espinay.

Hébert did not have much time to enjoy his success. One winter, when he was 52 years old, he suffered a bad fall on the ice. He died on January 25, 1627, and was buried in the priests' cemetery.

We remember Louis Hébert as the first French settler, or *habitant*. He was the first European to make his living in this country as a farmer. Hébert understood how important it was to cultivate the land, and how it would make New France independent. He set a standard for all the people who would follow.

Marie-Anne Gaboury
A Voyageur's Wife

Marie-Anne Gaboury was born in the summer of 1780 near Trois-Rivières, Quebec. She grew up to be a lively young woman, but by the time she was 25 it might have seemed she would never marry. After all, for 11 years she had appeared quite content to be the assistant housekeeper for the parish priest at St. Joseph's Church.

But her family knew a different Marie-Anne. She was beautiful, with bright blue eyes and blond hair. Full of life and intelligent, Marie-Anne had too much spirit to settle down to a quiet existence in the village of Maskinongé. She had been waiting for something or someone different.

On a winter evening in 1805, that someone walked into her life.

He was Jean-Baptiste Lagimodière, a 26-year-old fur trapper and buffalo hunter who had returned to Trois-Rivières from the west. When the parish found out, they invited him to speak at a gathering in their hall. He told them exciting tales of adventure about his years as a voyageur for the North West Company, and of his work as a hunter and trapper. Dressed from head to toe in otter, buckskin and caribou, Jean-Baptiste was probably the most interesting man Marie-Anne had ever met.

They were married on April 21, 1806, at St. Joseph's Church.

Marie-Anne Gaboury expected to spend her married life working with her husband on the family farm. But Jean-Baptiste was no farmer. He was a woodsman, fully intending to disappear into the wilderness for months to hunt and trap, leaving his wife behind to keep house and raise the children. When he told her that he was once again heading for the west, Marie-Anne made her decision. She would come along, and nothing Jean-Baptiste said could change her mind.

In the company of other voyageurs, Marie-Anne Gaboury and her husband travelled west to Pembina on the Red River. While crossing Lake Superior in huge freight canoes, the party was struck by two terrible storms. One canoe overturned and some of the men drowned. It was a wild and difficult journey for someone unused to it, but Marie-Anne was willing to suffer whatever was necessary to remain with her husband.

Two long months later they arrived at the fur trading post at Pembina, where they set up camp in a tent. Here Marie-Anne learned something that upset her terribly. Jean-Baptiste already had a wife — a Native wife. And they had three Métis children, girls who were half French and half Cree.

Many voyageurs had Native wives. It was harder to survive in the wilderness without a woman at your side. A Native wife cooked for her husband, repaired his clothing and made moccasins for him. She made his pemmican from fat, berries and dried buffalo meat. She could even act as a translator.

But the law did not recognize Jean-Baptiste's

Cree wife and three daughters as his legal family. The situation was very distressing for both women, so Jean-Baptiste took Marie-Anne to a new camp over 60 kilometres away. Unfortunately, no one knows for certain what happened to his Cree family.

Marie-Anne and Jean-Baptiste moved back to the trading post when she became pregnant, and with the help of the women there, her first child was born in 1807. They called the baby Reine (queen), because she arrived on January 6, the day the three kings visited the Christ child. That spring the little family set out for Edmonton House. Jean-Baptiste had decided to trap for the Hudson's Bay Company, which had offered to pay him more than the North West Company.

Marie-Anne Gaboury began to travel the country with her husband when he trapped and hunted. She often caused quite a stir when they went into Native camps, since she was the first white female the Native people had seen. Although she lived as her husband did, Marie-Anne always dressed as a French woman. She even carried a flatiron with her wherever she went, so she could press her wrinkled clothing.

One summer, again pregnant, she was riding with Jean-Baptiste across the prairie. Reine was in a cradleboard at her mother's side. Suddenly Marie-Anne's horse spied a herd of buffalo. Because it had been ridden in the hunt before, in its excitement the horse began to gallop, with Marie-Anne unable to control it. Jean-Baptiste managed to stop the animal, and a few hours later their second child was born, right there on the open prairie. He was nicknamed Laprairie.

The next spring they were captured by Sarcees. Marie-Anne and Jean-Baptiste managed to escape on horseback during the night with their two children. They rode hard for five days. Once they were back at the fort, Marie-Anne saw that the

Sarcees had been pursuing them the entire distance. They had barely made it.

There were four Lagimodière children by 1812. Marie-Anne Gaboury knew that her days of following her husband were over. Now she would remain in their shack at Red River. The place had changed since she first came out west. Nearly 200 people lived here now, and more would continue to come.

In 1818 Jean-Baptiste built her a log house at what was now called the Red River settlement. Happily, all of Marie-Anne and Jean-Baptiste's eight children survived their harsh childhoods. Seven of them settled in the area near their parents. Although Marie-Anne loved all of them, it seems that one daughter, Julie, was her favourite. Julie married a Métis man called Louis Riel. In time, they became the parents of a baby boy that they also named Louis. This boy went on to become a great Métis leader.

Marie-Anne Gaboury died when she was 95 years old. During her lifetime, she saw many changes in the west. Enormous herds of buffalo gave way to planted fields of wheat, and farming replaced the fur trade. Adapting to all these changes, she remained the one thing she had been from the start – a true pioneer.

John Crysler
A Loyalist Settler

John Crysler was 10 years old the first time he marched off to war.

His family were peace-loving people. In fact, when his grandparents had come to settle in the colony of New York in 1710, it was to escape a war in Germany. They had had to change their name from Greisler to Crysler so people could spell and pronounce it, but that was a small price to pay to live in safety.

When John was born, in 1770, the thick forests and plowed fields around Schoharie, New York, were quiet places. His parents, Philip and Elizabeth, had a productive homestead. A blacksmith's shop stood on their 20-hectare farm, and the crops they grew fed them and their children. They were a close family, with aunts, uncles and cousins all having farms nearby. Then the Cryslers' peace ended.

Some people believed that New York and the other colonies should no longer belong to England. They thought that people should be able to run their farms and businesses without paying heavy taxes to a king and country far across the Atlantic. These Patriots wanted independence. In 1776 they declared that the Thirteen Colonies would become the United States of America, and the Revolutionary War began.

But not everyone wanted to separate from England. Like others, the Cryslers were Loyalists. John's family took shelter at Fort Niagara, and the men joined a group called Butler's Loyal Rangers. In 1780 John and his 12-year-old brother Geronimus became drummer boys. With the Loyalists' Mohawk allies, the Crysler men fought against the Patriots. Homes and crops were burned. Many people on both sides died.

The war ended, a treaty was signed in 1783, and peace came to the United States. There was no peace for John's family or the other Loyalists, though. Their neighbours had not forgotten the attacks and the fighting. The United States government seized the Cryslers' property, and so the next year, they abandoned their home and set out for Canada, a British colony. John was 14 years old.

Leaving most of their possessions behind, John's family and thousands of other Loyalists made the hard journey to Montreal and then to Johnstown. The surveyors who went ahead of them measured out land along the St. Lawrence River into townships that they named after King George's children. This region would eventually be called Upper Canada. John's father applied to the government

Loyalist pioneers crossing a stream, Ontario

for a grant of land, and in 1787 the Cryslers settled at Williamsburgh. As young as they were, John and his brother also received land grants.

It was very difficult in the beginning. The government gave the Loyalists supplies to help them get started and plant crops. Slowly the Cryslers rebuilt their lives. John worked with his family in the fields. He helped build the simple cabin that was probably their first home in Canada.

When John became a man, he knew that he needed a wife by his side to help him run his farm and keep house.

Unhappily, his first two wives died, leaving him with several children. John Crysler's third wife, Nancy Finkle, lived a long life with him, and together they had many more children. Crysler farmed his land, and he opened a store. The family built a sawmill for lumber and a gristmill for flour. He was a busy, successful man who owned a great deal of land and a large, comfortable house.

The peace for which the Loyalists had sacrificed so much did not last. In 1812, when Britain and the United States went to war against each other, Canada remained loyal to England. So did John Crysler.

Canada had to be defended. Crysler had stayed active in the military, as a captain in the local militia. He was now often away with his men. This was hard on his family, since it meant that his wife and children had to look after the farm and businesses.

John Crysler's yellow-painted farmhouse became the British army's headquarters. On November 11, 1813, a battle was fought on his land, while his wife and some of the children hid in the root cellar of

their farmhouse. This was the Battle of Crysler's Farm. Although they were outnumbered, the British soldiers and militia fought well, and the American troops retreated. Crysler was sent to Montreal with news of the battle.

John Crysler's farm was at peace again, but once more, the price was high. Many soldiers had been killed. The house and barns were turned into hospitals for the wounded. It did not take long for the Cryslers' supplies to dwindle, with the army using them. The field had been trampled during the battle, and their crop was ruined. John's fine house was badly damaged. He appealed to the government for help, listing 400 pounds (about $2200) in damages. The government came to his aid.

After the War of 1812, John Crysler's lumber and flour mills became even more important to the family. A village called Crysler grew up around those mills, and John eventually moved there.

Throughout his life Crysler continued to serve his community. As a Justice of the Peace, he heard court cases in the local tavern, since there was no courthouse. In 1807 he was appointed as one of the trustees of the new public schools in the region. He even served as a member of the House of Assembly of Upper Canada.

In 1838, for the third time in his life, John Crysler went to war to defend his home. Rebels and their leader, William Lyon Mackenzie, believed that Upper Canada should break away from Britain. Crysler was appointed a lieutenant-colonel in the militia. He led his men — many of whom had also fought in the War of 1812 — to the town of Prescott, to successfully drive away the rebels. He was 68 years old, but still as loyal as he had always been.

John Crysler died in 1852, a Loyalist to the end. He is buried in the Anglican cemetery at Crysler.

Susanna Moodie

A Gentlewoman in Upper Canada

In 1813, Reydon Hall had been nestled in the English countryside for 130 years. The large attics and mysterious cellars of the old manor house were perfect for a 10-year-old's games. It was here that Susanna Strickland spent her childhood.

While her two younger brothers went away to school, Susanna and her five older sisters did not. Instead, Thomas and Elizabeth Strickland educated their daughters at home. There was a library filled with books, and on fine days the fields and the seaside beckoned.

Red-haired, unruly Susanna was very close to her sister Catharine. They shared a keen interest in poetry, history, theatre and nature. But perhaps the thing they had most in common was their love of writing.

When their father died in 1818, they were only 15 and 16 years old. Life changed. Susanna and

Catharine, like three of their other sisters, began to write with the idea of earning a living. In 1819 Catharine published a story for children. Susanna's first children's book was published in 1822. So began the professional writing careers of the two young ladies.

Susanna moved to London in 1830. The next year she married a retired British army officer and writer named John Moodie. The couple rented a small house not far from Reydon Hall, and Katie, their first child, was born. Though they were happy, there was no future for the Moodies in England. They thought about emigrating to Upper Canada. Susanna's brother Samuel was living in the Peterborough region, and the letters he sent home were encouraging. Though Susanna had her doubts – nothing in life had prepared her to be a pioneer – plans were begun.

But before Susanna and her family were to set sail, Catharine announced that she, too, was going to marry a retired army officer, Thomas Traill. In 1832 they left England to settle in Canada.

Susanna Moodie and her family soon followed. The nine-week crossing on the brig *Anne* was not

pleasant. Susanna was seasick, the food was poor and there was a water shortage. When the ship finally docked at Grosse-Île, Susanna was horrified by the chaos of hundreds of new immigrants. The brig continued on to Montreal, and from there, the Moodies journeyed by stagecoach and steamer to Cobourg in Upper Canada.

Susanna Moodie was not happy there in a house that resembled "a cattle-shed or pig-sty." Living far from her sister Catharine, she found her American neighbours unwelcoming. They considered Susanna a bluestocking, a woman too interested in books and learning.

She and John decided to homestead in the wilderness near Catharine's family and Samuel. And so in February of 1834, the Moodies endured an 18-hour sleigh ride to the Traills' new home on the shore of Lake Katchawanooka. Susanna wrote later, "I gazed through tears at the singularly savage scene around me, and secretly marvelled, 'What brought me here?'"

John Moodie knew this life would be a challenge for his wife; there was a second baby girl now. But it helped that Susanna could enjoy her sister's company while he supervised the work on

An early Canadian log house

their own log cabin. And when they moved to their own home, Catharine's was only a kilometre and a half away.

Susanna Moodie found she had a different sort of neighbour now. Here in the bush, people worked together. The men helped each other clear the land and build homes. The women delivered each other's babies, made herbal medicines and shared the burden of sick children. In such isolation, it was the only way for people to survive.

In 1837 there were rebellions in Upper and Lower Canada, and John Moodie joined the militia. As an officer, he was away from the farm for months at a time. With four children to care for – there were now two little boys as well – Susanna struggled to manage. Her neighbours and family were helpful, but it was difficult without John.

Still, Susanna proved resourceful. That bitterly cold February, the roof of the cabin caught fire. As "large pieces of burning pine began to fall through

the boarded ceiling," she dragged bureau drawers up a nearby hill, lined them with blankets, and bundled the children in to wait for help to arrive.

During the Moodies' years on their homestead, Susanna learned to make eel stew and dandelion coffee. She endured harsh winters, terrible summer heat and a devastating whirlwind. She was later to write, "When things come to the worse, they generally mend."

This was not the case with their farm. Although the countryside was beautiful, the soil was poor and the crops had been disappointing. In 1839 John moved Susanna and the children to Belleville. Their years in the bush were over.

The town of Belleville, as it appeared in 1830

Susanna Moodie did not put her experiences behind her. She had published some poems and short stories during those years. In 1836 her sister Catharine had managed to publish a book, *The Backwoods of Canada.* With John working as county sheriff, Susanna was now ready to write about her own years in

Goldfinch and Thistle,
by Susanna Moodie (1869)

the wilderness. *Roughing It in the Bush: Life in Canada* was published in England in 1852.

Susanna never became wealthy. After John resigned as sheriff in 1863, she sold paintings of flowers. It took years, but in 1871 *Roughing It in the Bush* was at last published in Canada.

Susanna Moodie died a widow in 1885, leaving behind her sister Catharine, five surviving children, and many grandchildren. She also left her stories, novels, poems and paintings. Thanks to her, we have a clear picture of the sacrifices made by gentlewomen who chose to come to Canada as pioneers, and rough it in the bush.

A poster promoting western immigration (ca. 1890)

Wasyl Eleniak

A Prairie Homesteader

In 1891, Canada was a country with close to five million people living mainly in Ontario, Quebec and the Maritimes. For its size, that was not a large population. The Canadian Pacific Railway had been finished in 1885, and the country was linked from the Atlantic to the Pacific. Huge areas of good prairie land out west were waiting for someone to homestead. All that was needed were the willing settlers.

Prime Minister Sir John A. Macdonald's government and the railway had a plan. They would send out advertisements to Great Britain and some other countries in Europe. If you came to Canada, you would get 160 acres (65 hectares) of land for next to nothing. All you had to do was get here.

Through German colonists, the news of this amazing offer reached Nebyliw in western Ukraine. For Wasyl Eleniak, it must have seemed like a miracle.

Wasyl was born in the village of Nebyliw on December 22, 1859, one of four children. The Eleniaks were extremely poor, with less than two hectares of land and a few animals. When his parents died, Wasyl, only 18 years old, became head of the family.

In 1883 he married Anna Roshko. Poverty meant that they had to live with Anna's parents, and in time their own children, Maria, Fedir and Magda, were born. Anna's dowry had consisted of less than two hectares of land, 100 crowns (about $40) and a cow. They worked hard to farm their land, and Wasyl worked as a logger. They both also laboured for the wealthy landowners. It was hard for Wasyl to bear the terrible conditions under which his wife had to toil, and he vowed to make a better life for them all. Seizing the chance, Wasyl Eleniak and two other men from the village decided to travel to Canada to see if the wonderful stories were true. The long years of work to achieve his goal had just begun.

The three men set off for Hamburg, Germany, where a ship waited. Only Eleniak and one of his companions had the 150 crowns necessary to cross the border. Their friend was turned back. At Hamburg they registered as labourers on the passenger list of the SS *Oregon*. It took them to Liverpool, England, and 11 days later, on September 7, 1891, they reached Montreal. The two Ukrainians stepped onto Canadian soil.

The men made their way by train out to Winnipeg. They were taken to Langenburg, and then to Calgary, by a land agent so that they could see the countryside for themselves. It was clear to them that what they had been told was true. There was more fertile land here than a person could ever want. Better still, in Canada there was political and religious freedom. The poverty they had known in Ukraine would be left behind. Back in Winnipeg, they each put down $10 on land at Langenburg.

Needing work and money so that they could bring their families over, they helped a Mennonite farmer thresh the wheat on his farm at Gretna, Manitoba. For this they were each paid $1.50 a day. By 1893, when Wasyl Eleniak had saved $220, he made the long journey back to Nebyliw for Anna and the children. Short of money for the return trip to Canada, he worked for two months floating log rafts downriver. Finally, on June 25, 1894, he was able to reach Canada with his wife and children, bringing two other families with them.

Homesteading involved more than just the free land. You needed horses, a plow, seed and many supplies. Eleniak worked for four more years as a herdsman for the Mennonites at Gretna, saving his money, still dreaming of his own farm. They called him the "cowboy Lemko" or Ukrainian cowboy. By then he had decided against settling at Langenburg. Instead, with his brother's family who had also now immigrated, he loaded all the family possessions into a railway boxcar heading for the Edna settlement at Chipman, Alberta. They had cloth to make clothing for the children, some hams, and flour. There were also 2 cows, 2 oxen, 30 chickens, a wagon and a plow. It was 1898. They were ready to homestead at last.

Wasyl Eleniak and his family grew cereal crops. They had poultry, milk cows and a vegetable garden.

They raised cattle and horses, of which Wasyl was very fond. He had a real talent for breaking wild horses, and soon had them tame and gentle. He never owned a tractor of his own. Instead, he was partner with some of his neighbours in the ownership of a steam-powered tractor and thresher.

Eleniak became a successful homesteader, eventually expanding his farm to 260 hectares. Active in the community, he was considered a good neighbour and a good family man. When he died in 1956 at the age of 96, four generations of Eleniaks lived on – in 7 surviving children, 51 grandchildren, 62 great-grandchildren and one great-great grandchild.

Two hundred thousand Ukrainians immigrated to Canada between 1896 and 1914, willing to work hard and make huge sacrifices to live in this country. They brought a rich culture that remains today. When the Canadian Citizenship Act became law in 1947, Wasyl Eleniak was one of the first people, and the first Ukrainian, to receive his Citizenship Certificate. He accepted it proudly, for himself and for all Ukrainians.

A photograph of Wasyl Eleniak, taken by Yousef Karsh
the day after they both became Canadian citizens (1947)